Publishing Children's Poetry For 19 Years

Bust-A-Rhyme

Giving verse
a voice

Verses From England

Edited By Aimée Vanstone

First published in Great Britain in 2010 by:

 Young**Writers**

Young Writers
Remus House
Coltsfoot Drive
Peterborough
PE2 9JX
Telephone: 01733 890066
Website: www.youngwriters.co.uk

Foreword

Young Writers' Bust-A-Rhyme competition is a showcase for secondary school pupils to share their poetic creativity and inspiration. Selecting the poems has been challenging and immensely rewarding. The effort and imagination invested by these young writers makes their poems a pleasure to enjoy reading time and time again.

Young Writers was established in 1991 to nurture creativity in our children and young adults, to give them an interest in poetry and an outlet to express themselves. Seeing their work in print will encourage them to keep writing and become our poets of tomorrow.

Contents

Maltings Academy, Witham

Mecklenburg Pupil Referral Unit, Kingston-upon-Thames

Newlands Girls' School, Maidenhead

St Dominic's School, Brewood

The Crest Girls' Academy, London

Wreake Valley Community College, Leicester

The Poems

My World!

I have a little world where everything is good,
Where I go at night and walk among the wood.
To everyone else it's just a fantasy,
But it's very real for me.
There are trees of candy, and little muffins.
My world is really something.
In the day the sun is shining,
At night the sun is nigh
And the trees are really high.
Then I wake up in my bed
And realise it's all inside my head!

Kally Elson (12)
Astor College for the Arts, Dover

The Plane Journey!

The airport wasn't that far
As we went in my dad's car.
We went past Sandwich Bay,
It was a blue sky that day.
As I got on the plane,
The hostess was standing there with a cane.
I sat down in my seat,
I could smell the dinner, veg and meat. *Yuck!*
Take-off was so great,
We went so fast we could be late.
Eating Pringles from the pot,
There were two left and Mum said, 'That's your lot.'
As I hopped off the plane I found a road,
Walked down there happy as can be,
It was really hot and sunny,
I was at the sea!

Tahlia Gilbert (12)
Astor College for the Arts, Dover

Ellie's World

People always laugh,
But I know it's true,
Because when I'm in the bath,
I dream, dream far away.
I'm in a vortex first
And then I arrive.
I jump the strawberries
Of my milkshake life,
I go to my fruit
And to eat them all through,
But I'll save some for later
As my tummy's getting fatter.
Next I'll go to the skyscrapers,
I'll get everything I want.
It's open till late,
So I'll shop till I drop.
That is my world,
I love it so much,
Who knows where it will end?

Ellie Stone (12)
Astor College for the Arts, Dover

America!

A dventures every day
M agnificent sights
E verlasting fun to enjoy
R ides!
I nteresting shows
C elebrations
A mazing for everybody
N ever-ending fun

A nimal sections
M agical adventures
U nforgettable memories
S creaming for the rides
E very day fun
M assive prizes
E xtreme adventures
N ew rides
T allest rides

P eople laughing
A dvertisments
R eady, set, go!
K ids
S miles all around!

Charlie Spiers (12)
Astor College for the Arts, Dover

France

I like snails, yes I do,
Why don't you come and try one too?
Come along to France, where romance is high,
And enjoy one of our freshly-baked pies.

Come to France and you will see
The frogs jumping in glee.
Come and enjoy a freshly-baked baguette,
It is mouth-wateringly good,
You won't have tasted anything like it yet.

Kyran Chalmers (13)
Astor College for the Arts, Dover

My Journey

There's lots of ways to travel afar,
By motorbike, plane, horse or sleigh on the snow,
Even hop if it's not too far to go.

But my favourite way when there's someone to meet
Is the good old-fashioned use of my feet.

Sophie Carter (12)
Astor College for the Arts, Dover

Journey To Legoland

J oyful thoughts
O nly in my dreams
U nder my duvet waiting
R aring to go
N early time
E ventually we'll leave
Y ahoo! We're on our way!

T iring trip
O nly an hour to go

L egoland, at last we're here!
E xciting rides greet my eyes
G reat fun to be had
O ver the moon, I'm going mad
L ego models I love to hold
A fter a ride, time to eat
N ever want to leave
D arn, it's over. Time to go!

Brandyn Richardson (12)
Astor College for the Arts, Dover

Devon

D evon is a magnificent place
E xciting and enjoyable it seems to be
V ery big the beaches seem
O n a daily basis I think about Devon and the
N ever-ending fun!

B est sport for me
O n the beach
D evon
Y ellow sun
B odyboarding is great fun!
O n sizzling sand
A mazing waves
D oing what I think is best
I n the sea it's as cold as ice
N o boring times
G reat fun!

Ellie Smith (12)
Astor College for the Arts, Dover

Space

5, 4, 3, 2, 1, I'm crying like a baby,
I'm sucking my thumb.
Quick everybody, run, run, run,
You're going to miss all the fun, fun, fun!
The colours are red and green,
They make the rocket tall and lean.
Hold on! It's going to be a bumpy ride.
Does anyone know where I can hide?
Into space we *whoosh,*
My brain has turned to mush.
To the window to see the sight,
Who knows whether it's day or night?
Smell burning, rockets turning, stars and moons
All in lines like platoons.
Oh how I love to go to space
And feel the cold moonlight on my face.

Bethany Robinson (12)
Astor College for the Arts, Dover

Romania

R omania is a wonderful place
O radea, the city in which I stayed
M any fields of sunflowers
A cres and acres of corn
N ew buildings all around
I ntense heat all day
A thousand miles away from home.

Jamie Howgill (12)
Astor College for the Arts, Dover

Turkey

T wo weeks in the sun
U nder the palm trees we relaxed
R unning to get into the swimming pool
K eeping ourselves away from the burning sun
E ating the figs we picked off the trees
Y et our holiday ended, but we will be back soon!

Cassia Barkes (12)
Astor College for the Arts, Dover

Flying

Flying
Flying low
Coming down quick
Just waiting to land
The tyres screech
Going fast
Landed!

Matt Ripley (12)
Astor College for the Arts, Dover

The Boat Journey

The horn shouted as I looked out of the porthole
At the hundreds of ants scurrying aboard.
I could hear the waves as they crashed and roared.
As the great white ship set sail across the sea,
Titanic, I was thinking and the massive tragedy.
That night the boat was rocking,
I couldn't get to sleep,
I tossed and turned all through the night,
I even counted sheep.
The boat was docking at its final destination,
All the people waiting, I could taste anticipation.
The boat journey has now ended,
It was gone so quick,
Quicker than the speed of light,
Tick-tock, tick-tock, tick!

Connor Tagg
Astor College for the Arts, Dover

Gran Canaria

G reetings to this paradise
R ain it does not often
A ir is clean and pure
N ine times a week there's a barbecue on the beach

C old it never is
A nd let's go to the water park
N ever again am I going down that massive slide!
A nother glistening day at the beach
R adiant, gleaming faces enjoying their stay
I t has a lot of interest
A nother beautiful day in paradise.

Jake Smith (12)
Astor College for the Arts, Dover

Down To The Gym

Down to the gym I do go
With my mum, I love it so.
Onto the treadmill I do get,
I am able to run without getting wet.
Next to the bike,
Do a mile hike.
To the running machine next,
My muscles I do need to flex.
My heart is pumping,
The music is jumping.
Onto the cross-trainer, I try my best,
I run for ten minutes then I rest.
I have some water, they advise you to,
I make sure I listen to what they say and do.
Hayley, the trainer, teaches me the rules,
I am tired now and sweaty too.
I will give it a rest now,
So I will say bye to you.

Emmy Billing (12)
Astor College for the Arts, Dover

North Pole

Off to the North Pole I shall go,
Where there is lots of snow.
Can't forget my winter socks,
Mind out for those rocks.
As I glide down the icy ramps
Past all the camps,
I can hear the polar bears roaring
And penguins snoring.
Now I am off to bed
To rest my weary head!

Jessica Glasgow (12)
Astor College for the Arts, Dover

Heaven

Heaven can be anything you want it to be,
Depending what you want to see.
Every time I sit and sigh,
I see clouds floating by.

Every time I see a star
I think of my loving grampa.
When I see the pearly gate,
I hope it's not tempted to my fate
And I wish it to be a long wait.

When the beautiful angel sings,
She flies around with her beautiful wings.
Oh look, there's cloud eleven.
No it's not, it's the stairway to Heaven.

Holly-Louise Mackie (12)
Astor College for the Arts, Dover

Egypt

The place where the pyramids stand tall,
Where there is hot sand and a market stall.
It's not a place which is busy,
It's the heat which makes you dizzy.
Tombs as dark as space,
Feeling the sunburn on your face.
Mummies that scare you in the night,
The feeling that you get when you wish it were light.
The sun: a ball of gas in the sky,
Hanging so gracefully and high.
Watching the camels walking on hot sand,
Whilst listening to an Egyptian band.
We're having fun, we like it a lot,
Wish you were here (or maybe not).
Well then, I have to go,
Next time we're going to Alaska,
Where they have mountains of snow.

Kimberley Bonham (12)
Astor College for the Arts, Dover

My Sweet Planet

M y sweet planet
Y oung people enjoy sweets with lots of sugar

S o tasteful and sweet
W onderful licking lollies
E veryone loves my sweet planet
E ating apples everyone loves
T alking and giggling away

P laying and having fun
L aying on the best pink fluffy pillows
A lways be happy, you have to be
N ever to be sad
E very day shall be the best
T hat's my sweet planet!

Tiffany Marlow (12)
Astor College for the Arts, Dover

The Beach!

Here I am at the beach,
The sun's so near it's in my reach.
Sandy towels and wet toes,
I slap on my suncream as the temperature grows.
Smiles on faces wherever I go,
Right, left, high and low.
Hurray! The ice cream man is here at last,
So all the children run so fast.
Look over here and see what I've made,
A sandcastle with a bucket and spade.
The calming sounds of the sea,
The waves breathe so gently
As I lay down facing the sky,
Not a fluffy cloud passes by.
I run my fingers through the fine sand,
Suddenly I can see my hand.
It's time to put my things away,
So I can use them again someday.
Tomorrow I'll be out to play.

Katie Misson (12)
Astor College for the Arts, Dover

Seasons

S un is shining
P etals smell so nice
R ivers are running
I n spring the flowers come out
N ow we hear the birds singing
G reen grass looking so bright

S ky so bright, sun so hot
U mbrellas up on the beach
M um puts on the suncream
M um makes us wear our hats
E njoying picnics
R oads are packed with cars

A utumn is when I go back to school
U mbrellas keep us dry
T rees' leaves turn brown and fall
U p in the trees birds are nesting
M ist and fog are about
N o one is coming out

W arm fires
I nside and get ready for bed
N early time to travel
T rees are covered in snow
E njoying sleep
R ain and thunder is about.

Keyleigh Stevenson (12)
Astor College for the Arts, Dover

The World

T he world is a perfect place!
H appy places to visit and
E verywhere is unique.

W onders and adventures
O f different countries.
R ound and round the world spins
L ike a
D isco ball, bright and colourful.

Sophie Ryan (12)
Astor College for the Arts, Dover

My Day In Disneyland

Mickey Mouse jumping up and down,
Kids with chocolate all over their faces,
Parents carrying heavy cases through the giant tower,
We finally go home, then silence!
Peace at last.
The perfect paradise day.

Emma Letts (12)
Astor College for the Arts, Dover

Italy, Pizza

Pizza, pizza, cooked with a thick crust,
It looks as flat as a pancake.
Sometimes pizza could come out
Like the colours of a rainbow.
Cheese on a pizza has melted
Like chocolate in the sun.
Pizzas taste like the wonders of the world.
Stuffed crust when you finish a delicious pizza.
You can get different delicious flavours
Like pepperoni, meat feast etc.
When it comes to me
It demands me to eat it!

George Gittos (12)
Astor College for the Arts, Dover

Egypt

The mummies are as white as a ghost,
The tombs are dark like the sky at night,
The sand is hot and yellow like the sun,
The pyramids are as brown as a brick,
The camels' humps are like bumps in the road.

Katie Medhurst (12)
Astor College for the Arts, Dover

Japan

J oy is in Japan

A nimation is drawn such as Manga

P eople speak different languages like Japanese

A nimals live in Japan as animals live in our country

N ow you know what Japan is like!

Nathan Keeble (12)
Astor College for the Arts, Dover

Cake On A Train

They spent all night making it, then I just ate it.
I ran all around, up and down in a wild manner.
Oh so nice, sugar and spice, that's what it was made of,
All covered in icing, all over the train.
I got there, it was gone!

Georgia Walker (12)
Astor College for the Arts, Dover

New York

The sun is in your eyes
As you say your goodbyes.
You hold onto your loved ones tight,
Wondering if your decision is right.
As you walk onto the plane
It starts to rain
And it reminds you of your pain.
Your whole life has gone down the drain.
The sun is out
And that's what it's all about.
It's a new day
At New York Bay.
I'm having fun
Now the hard work's done.

Holly Walton (12)
Astor College for the Arts, Dover

28

Hermione Granger

Harry Potter's best friend,
Only one who knows all the tricks.
Muggles are what her family are,
Intelligence beyond imagination,
Never without her wand.
In class she loves to work,
Everyone wants to be like her.

Good with magic,
Rather smart when it comes to magic.
A good friend to Harry and Ron.
Never uses the wrong spell,
Great with her mind,
Everyone's friend,
Right every time!

Micky Mills (11)
Astor College for the Arts, Dover

Iraq

Crawling around the trenches,
Climbing over fences,
We're trying to beat Iraq,
But we keep getting blown back.
We're trying to dodge their bullets
But we don't succeed,
That's why so many people are dying these days.
Sometimes I just hope it's a phase.

Tyler Lee (14)
Astor College for the Arts, Dover

Horses

H oof picking
O at eating
R iding through the woods
S addle shining
E ager to canter
S traw jumping.

Abbie Winfield (12)
Astor College for the Arts, Dover

Untitled

Packing all my stuff,
Getting in the car,
Opening my window,
Bugging my sister,
Travelling is fun.
Mum, I need to wee.
Stopping at the gas station,
Getting something to eat.
We are nearly there,
It's going to be great.
We are here at last,
My legs really hurt
So I run around,
My sister does too.
My uncle says,
'My, haven't you grown.'

Stephanie Harcourt-Ronaldson (12)
Astor College for the Arts, Dover

The Wonderful World Of Devon

Balcony jumping
Pod playing
Swimming, diving
Clothes shopping
Friends meeting
Sun burning
Tor rising
Candy smelling
TV watching.

Harley Jones (12)
Astor College for the Arts, Dover

Spain - Haiku

Hot sun shining down
Swimming in the pool all day
I love Spain, it rules.

Kieran Taylor (12)
Astor College for the Arts, Dover

Spain

S ing as well as I can
P eople laughing happily and jumping with joy
A nd making friends is so much fun
I nside dancing like mad
N ever-ending fun.

Madie Jones (13)
Astor College for the Arts, Dover

Florida's Place

F eeling the real 3D movies
L ots of excitement and places to explore
O ther adventures to seek
R ides to experience
I t's a good family holiday
D oing lots of fun stuff
A nd seeking your loveable characters.

Jordan Tuner (12)
Astor College for the Arts, Dover

Owen S

Bike riding
Big Mac eating
Football playing
Nose picking
Pool swimming
Xbox playing
Bebo loving
MSN chatting
Sport playing
Mates calling.

Liam Smith (11)
Astor College for the Arts, Dover

Kate Beckinsale

Actress from England,
Stars in fabulous films,
Eyes shine as bright as diamonds.
Sitting under the bright sunset
Thinking where her life will take her next.
Acting round from here to there,
Sharing her dreams with those who seem to care.
Her black hair sparkles in the moonlight.

Amy West (11)
Astor College for the Arts, Dover

All About Heather

Bob the Builder watching
Photo taking
Facebook loving
Friend playing
Pasta eating
Brother hating
Food tasting
Poster collector
Plate licker
Silly dancer
Music listener
Face puller.

Emma Williams (11)
Astor College for the Arts, Dover

Heather's The Weird Girl

H appy all day
E very day laughing
A lways on the computer
T ired in the morning
H yper as you could ever imagine
E ating all day
R ushing around

S illy and funny with her brother
U nbelievably wacky
C hatting all the time
H ungry all the time

If you meet Heather, be warned,
She'll freak you out!

Heather Such (11)
Astor College for the Arts, Dover

40

Ryan Sheckler

R oaring
Y oung
A ce
N ot afraid

S uper
H appy
E xtreme
C harged
K icked
L ifted
E ating
R ealistic.

Liam Clark (11)
Astor College for the Arts, Dover

Harry Potter

H arry is a wizard
A nd he has a broomstick
R on is his friend
R onald Weasley is his real name
Y ay, Griffindor wins

P otter has a scare
O n the pitch he flies his broomstick
T op of the sky he flies
T o catch the Golden Snitch
E xtra friends
R ushing through the sky.

Alexandra Vladimirou (11)
Astor College for the Arts, Dover

Lilli

L ike my best friend
I s the one who has the cutest horse
L illi is the funny one of the lot of us
L azy, I don't think so, bonkers is the right word
I n my house all the time.

Jade Van-Dyke-Hempenstall (11)
Astor College for the Arts, Dover

Me

My name is Chloe Smith,
I go to Astor College for the Arts.
Family Guy is funny! Ha, ha, ha.
A go on the computer? Yes please.
I love chocolate!
Primark for bargains.
JD is the place to be for me.
Yeah, boy, music rules!
Whoop, whoop!

Chloe Smith (11)
Astor College for the Arts, Dover

Nathan

Animal loving
Lego building
Noodle eating
Jake and Josh watching
Football playing
Bike rider
Dirt digging
Outside rounders
Art drawing
Family, grandparents.

Chad Humphries (11)
Astor College for the Arts, Dover

Feelings

In my childhood, I lived this selfish kind of love.
Wherever I would go,
My face was always a disgrace to the world.
I would always see my man in the mirror,
This man would be someone
That would look evil to the world.
I would always say . . .
Before you judge, try hard to love.
Look within your heart
Then ask, 'Have you seen my childhood?'

So I'm gonna make a change in my life,
It's gonna feel so good,
And gonna make it right.
I've been a victim of this
Selfish kind of love.
But today's where I make love
To one and all.
I've always been a judgement
Of my colour and race, this is the way
My life leads into disgrace.

Beat me, hate me,
You can never break me.
My body is strong as steel.
I'm tired of being the victim of hate,
The only friends that I have
Are my brothers and sisters,
But I don't care if I am black or white.

I will always be strong,
But sometimes in life
We don't want to see,
But if Martin Luther was living,
This wouldn't be.

Henna Mahmood (13)
Golden Hillock School, Birmingham

My Family

Sometimes happy, sometimes sad,
Altogether, we're not bad.
My family and I stick together,
We won't part, absolutely never.
Broken families can get back together
But there will always be a crack forever.
We are different, we are special,
And our hearts are not made of metal.
Brothers and sisters, we are close,
We always care for each other the most.
My family will always love each other,
We will always be there for one another.

Samiya Akhtar (12)
Golden Hillock School, Birmingham

What Is Life?

What is life to me?
I don't own a car,
I don't own a TV,
I don't own a bus pass,
But I'm free to be me.

What is life to me?
I go to school
'Cause I think it's cool,
I'm smart, I'm intelligent,
But I'm not a fool.
I make good use of my time after school.

What is life to me?
I love to play games with my mate,
But I've been bullied since I was eight.
They bullied me because I'm black,
They bullied me because I'm white,
They bullied me 'cause I wasn't fat,
They bullied me 'cause I wasn't thin,
They bullied me 'cause I was something
They wanted to have been.
What is life?

Elisha Stokes (12)
Golden Hillock School, Birmingham

The Loss Of Mr Michael Jackson

My day started, seeing his face on the big black screen,
Happiness turned on him leaving the world to be mean.
I can still feel his innocent soul around this room,
Right now all I see is a dusty old broom.
A singing, dancing, genius star, who gave us all he had,
Such as 'Thriller', 'Billie Jean', 'Man in the Mirror' and 'Bad'.
Why, oh why was he snatched from me?
Oh how I wonder how he'll be.
Countless tears drop from my eyes
As I see the cruel jokes made against him, which are pure lies.
I still cry when I see his glimpse as my eyelid closes,
I won't ever forget him, never!
He might not be alive but he is in my heart forever,
My inspiration.
Michael Jackson, an angel sent from above,
Who taught us how to sing and dance,
He is in a deep trance.
Rest in peace my singing, dancing, genius.

Sadiyah Ahmed (13)
Golden Hillock School, Birmingham

We Should Care

Cars and factories are all harmful
We sit back, say life's full of fun
Why don't we stop and think about it
That we an all save the planet?

Cars and factories cause acid rain
But at the end of the day we are to blame
We sit in our cars always
Don't give a care any day
So why don't we help each other
By helping the environment
But doing it together?

Rosemina Ahmed (12)
Golden Hillock School, Birmingham

Life

Some things in life turn out bad
Which happens to make us feel sad.
Nothing's the same,
Every time I play a game.
You win and lose
And then just end up with a big bruise.
It's dark here, and there it's light
But nothing seems to turn out right,
Which makes me end up in a big fight.

Hena Begum (12)
Golden Hillock School, Birmingham

I Hate Life

I've been pushed around
I'd rather be locked up in a pound.

I walk to school with my head down
They push me, they hit me
In blood I drown
Struggling for help, people look and frown.

In my deathbed I lay
Nobody asks, 'Are you OK?'

So what can I do
Other than pray for me and you?

Hendah Hussein (12)
Golden Hillock School, Birmingham

Knife Crime

We don't make those sharp metal things
At this age they only care about shiny new bling
They roam around the streets with their heads held high
When deep down they know
They're carrying something that can make you cry.
They do it to be cool,
But they're just acting like fools,
Stabbing and jabbing with no care at all,
Families and friends who cannot bear the call.
Gangs with hoodies
They're not really your buddies
They know the consequences,
They might be locked up for life.
So don't ever carry that sharp, deadly knife,
Leave it at home, safe in a drawer,
Don't leave that poor soul dead on the floor.
Care for that one or he will soon be gone,
Stop knife crime in your hood
Before you see the cold red blood.

Sophie Kaur (13)
Golden Hillock School, Birmingham

3 O'Clock Kick Off

Walking through the stadium,
Hear the cheers,
Feel the crowds jumping,
See their tears.

As the referee blows the whistle,
The match suddenly starts,
The greatest game on Earth,
The chanting's off the chart.

With one-two passes,
Shots here and there,
The game is on fire,
You're riveted to your chair.

With teamwork the ball is shot
Deep into enemy grounds,
With a long ball across the pitch,
The right feet are found.

Number 9 takes control
As the through ball is set,
And like a flash of lightning,
The ball's behind the net.

With one last cheer
The game has come to an end,
As I walk out the gates,
Ending the perfect weekend.

Imamul Ahmed (12)
Golden Hillock School, Birmingham

Last Words!

Love, what a beautiful sight,
It gets annoying, is it wrong or right?
It's happened to you, it's happened to me,
It's clearly love, can't you see?
It's got you, it's in your head,
All you need to do is lie in your bed.
It's getting too hard, you let out that emotion,
You're not the only one, there's so much commotion.
You love her too much, it's tearing you apart,
You can't choose, you want to tear out your heart.
It's not possible, you don't have a choice,
You listen to that one thing people call a voice.
It's screaming and shouting and telling you there's hope,
You can't take it any more, you grab the nearest rope.
You tie it hard and give it a good pull,
All of a sudden you have the control of a bull!
It's final, you have made your decision,
You choose a knife with that utter, great precision.
You've done it, now you close your eyes,
The last words are heard before you rise.

Mohammed Shoaibzahid (13)
Golden Hillock School, Birmingham

55

A Special Friend

My friend, when I think of you
I think of all that we have been through
All the times we argue and fight
I know deep inside that it is not right
I'm getting better as the days go by
I wish I could never say such a big lie
My dear friend, I miss you a lot
I still wonder why I did this to you
Our friendship will never end
This is a promise from me to you, my friend
Friends till the end is what we will be
You are a friend that really cares
All my secrets that I can share
You are better than a sister can ever be
I feel so great when you meet me
Others stand by you when you are right
But I stand by you whenever you are wrong
This is a wish from me to you
You are a true friend that will never break up
I really wanted more friends
But you are enough for me
I was really happy until you left.

Huseena Latif (13)
Golden Hillock School, Birmingham

The Forgotten Soldiers

Bang, explosions, the soldier left for dead.
'Come on soldier, we're running out of time!'
Through the wild smoke above their injured heads,
Not very fair. He committed no crime.

I picked up my gun and cried at my loss.
He was a good lad, he shouldn't be gone!
Forget him, I thought, *listen to the boss,*
And just focus on the mission we're on.

These brave men and women sent far to fight,
Nothing to help but all the weapons they hold.
They want to call peace, the enemy might,
But what about the tales that can't be told?

Constant darkness followed by constant night,
One time that darkness will turn into light.

Ashleigh Tinkler (16)
Hartlepool Sixth Form College, Hartlepool

Four Beats: A Beat For Every Year

Battered, beaten, bruised, then all on my own,
My bruises hidden, a secret well kept.
Daddy doesn't do this when Mummy's home.
A smile on my face but my heart still wept.
Families are supposed to be together
Every bit of tension washed away,
Never apart, just loving forever,
A caring family, stuck together like clay.
One day Mum will see I'm hurting inside
And I can get away from this nightmare,
When I get off this roller coaster ride
To find someone that will love me and care.

All children are supposed to be cared for,
But somehow, my heart repeatedly tore.

Riley-Jayne Moodie (16)
Hartlepool Sixth Form College, Hartlepool

Monday

If there is one thing that I cannot stand,
And I'm probably not the only one,
It seems they're on a constant demand
To a place where our minds have gone.

The only thing I have to think about
Is why I'm not at home lying in bed,
Sleeping, like I should be, without a doubt.
No thinking, a pillow under my head.

And yet I know that I'm just dreaming on
And reality hits me like a bus.
So on my desk I lay my head upon,
Every time it's the same, for all of us.

So before I slump back into my daze,
Tell me why I *really* don't like Mondays.

Sarah-Elizabeth Lester (16)
Hartlepool Sixth Form College, Hartlepool

Chewing

Chewing food with your mouth open is bad,
Disgusting, awful, you make me feel sick.
It is not the most fun that can be had
Unless, of course, you are extremely thick.
Did your mother never show you good ways?
Unless you ungratefully ignored them?
Because my trustworthy friend there are days
When I could not care less about your phlegm.
Keep it closed and buttoned and zipped and tight,
Otherwise you will end up in trouble.
My good mate, you will end up in a fight,
Some mean guy will come and burst your bubble.
You'll not be able to chew any more,
Death will come along and knock on your door.

Joshua Timothy (16)
Hartlepool Sixth Form College, Hartlepool

The State Of Things

Tabloid tales of deceit and slander
Pollute our minds, with their agenda.
A plan to make society blander,
Elements in the cultural blender.
A tabloid sweetheart with a tarnished past
Reveals all in single camera flash.
15 minutes of fame will never last,
She will fall with a monumental crash.
While an oppressed civil libertine
Woos her with his boyish charms and wit,
She's got to be clean, she's got to be lean,
For the intoxicated dream to fit.
Die not with dignity, but in the public eye,
Advertise your death and a nation will cry.

Robert Ash (16)
Hartlepool Sixth Form College, Hartlepool

Music

When I look back at music, I can grin.
Sixties, eighties, noughties - every decade.
Thinking of Johnny Cash - sipping his gin.
When all the songs ended in a slow fade,
1969 - The Beatles' last gig
And Elvis Presley brought in rock 'n' roll,
When the Rolling Stones had been on a shindig.
The eighties' recession, I'm on the dole,
The Runaways with their short, shredding riffs.
The first girl rock band - I dig what they say,
Music brought the eighties' mullets and the quiffs.
Don't forget country tunes by Doris Day.
My favourite bands include these short few,
Guns 'n' Roses, Nirvana and The Who.

Anna Frostwick (16)
Hartlepool Sixth Form College, Hartlepool

Animal Testing

Enhancing a feature is not worth shame
Superficial views marked stop with a cross
Brought into the world to help solve blame
Last night's struggle to justify the loss.
Inferior species to help mankind
Airbrushed visions foresee a higher stand
Pain and unfairness to cure guilty minds
Impulse purchases brought closer to hand
Yet make-up and drugs cannot replace death
Unnecessary pleasures remain vain
Still animals killed leave the smallest mess
Daily existence contains too much pain.
The days seem endless, trapped in a small cage.
Still the creatures of God live sad, unstaged.

Serena Marley-Lawson (16)
Hartlepool Sixth Form College, Hartlepool

Drugs!

He is high again, I am losing it
He is lost in his own little world, alone
He can't even stand so he has to sit
I try ringing, he won't answer the phone

He goes round singing, people stop and stare
I do not know what to do any more
He buys any drug, he thinks they are rare
I have seen him inject, then fall on the floor

I don't know if he will make it today
I feel like I'm talking to no one
Who knows if he'll even make it till May
I know one day very soon he'll be gone

And now I wake up and he isn't there
I walk around alone, I feel so bare.

Jessica Spence (16)
Hartlepool Sixth Form College, Hartlepool

My Best Friend

It's because of her I'm here today
It's because of her I am who I am
She's my inspiration every day
She's the comfort blanket I call my mam
She's also known as my best friend
With her warming smile and endless love
All my problems she manages to mend
She's my angel sent from way up above
My helping hand at the end of each day
My guide when I need someone to lean on
Through thick and thin she will always stay
She holds back her tears so I see her strong.

She's all I have, all I will ever need
For her never to leave my side I plead.

Diane Hanson (16)
Hartlepool Sixth Form College, Hartlepool

The Destruction Of Family

The people feel cold though the sun beats down,
The casualty number rises day by day,
And still lifeless bodies scattered around,
Your brain says leave, but the contract says stay.

Life's not worth living if it's just to fight,
Men and women dying, it's not correct,
When they've got no reason and no real plight,
The life of their families needlessly wrecked.

As children cry at the graves of the dead,
Onlookers outraged at the pointless war,
Young women lie alone curled up in bed
And parents have lost the ones they adore.

So as for Iraq, I don't feel that it's right
To send someone out, guns blazing, to fight.

Laurence Brown (16)
Hartlepool Sixth Form College, Hartlepool

Family Life

My family means the world to me,
I have seven sisters and one brother.
I have my favourites, which are lovely.
Six of my siblings share the same mother.
My sisters are very similar,
My brother is shy and a loner.
My favourite sister is called Camilla.
My brother lives with his stepmam, Fiona.
Samantha is rich and has lots of cash,
My mam works hard to look after us all.
Caitlyn drives a big car and thinks she's flash,
My father I don't know, is very tall.
You now know about my family at home,
So now you can go and leave us alone.

Michaela Hope (16)
Hartlepool Sixth Form College, Hartlepool

Joy Rider's Capture

Lurking in groups in car parks together,
Teenagers gather to see what's for free.
If they're lucky, they'll keep it forever,
I notice there is no CCTV.
Our car's out there, but not for the taking,
Little did we know it would be stolen.
Younger new criminals in the making;
They came in and left the locker broken.
We found out they left with our car they'd claimed,
We sent a long complaint to the head boss,
But they insisted they couldn't be blamed.
However, they're 'sorry for our loss'.
Legal reasons prevent them being named,
So now we have learnt they cannot be shamed!

Samantha Grigg (16)
Hartlepool Sixth Form College, Hartlepool

Evanescent Hope

The young boy cowers in fear and cries,
Like the dog, chained, beaten and left alone.
A right hook strikes the boy and all hope dies,
Whilst the starving dog dreams of just a bone.

The defenceless boy meets drunken abuse;
The neglected dog meets cold loneliness.
Thrown against a railing, his blood gets loose,
Outside, hunger converts to grogginess.

It is the same for them, day in, day out,
As long nights progress, the neglect does too.
If the pair's safety is ever in doubt,
The abusers deny it, yet it's true!

Until this injustice is sorted out,
The dog and the boy just cower and pout.

Lewis Wood (16)
Hartlepool Sixth Form College, Hartlepool

Wimbledon

It's almost time for July to begin,
The sun is out and the racquets are new.
Can Roger compete and possible win?
Can anyone beat him? Only a few.
Now the umpires are at the ready,
Spectators will roar at any second.
Roger will serve, can he hold it steady?
Ball is called out, the ball boy is beckoned,
They need a break, it's forty-forty, deuce.
A shout from the crowd, 'Go Roger, you'll win.'
He tries to volley, the volley is loose,
It scrapes the line and the ball is called in.
Roger is the winner, he's on the ball,
His name is next to the greatest of all.

Caroline Huntley (16)
Hartlepool Sixth Form College, Hartlepool

It's Not For Girls?

Football for girls, or is it just for boys?
The referee checks the net for a hole,
The game has begun and what a loud noise,
A kick of the ball and nearly a goal.
It is a foul, who will take the free-kick?
The ball is received and put on the spot,
No one will take the kick, who will they pick?
The player gets the ball and makes a shot.
The game is over and no one has won,
A player was hurt and so was a fan.
The rain has stopped and out comes the sun,
Some of the teams have got a transfer ban.
It's a beautiful game, it's bitter and sweet,
It can be magical, even with some broken feet.

Rebecca Forrest (16)
Hartlepool Sixth Form College, Hartlepool

Water

There is simply not enough to go round
Suffering is caused and people will die
The food and water just cannot be found
It echoes around the world, we say, 'Why?'

The dirty water makes everyone ill
So aid workers fit all the pumps they can
But who is responsible for the bill?
Grants are there, but not enough for the plan.

They are forced to walk for miles every day
Hard ground underfoot and still miles to go
Only the horizon to lead the way
Containers are heavy as the winds blow.

We need to realise when we turn the tap
That their land is caught in a drought-filled trap.

Elizabeth Walker (16)
Hartlepool Sixth Form College, Hartlepool

An Ode To Chicken

Chicken wings are just so radical bro
I shall inform you of my poultry lust
I eat my chicken wings in pouring snow
Into my mouth, my chicken meal is thrust
Chicken is the holy food of the gods
Zeus ate chicken wings and breast every day
He caught his chickens from the Earth with rods
'Chicken is amazing,' is all he'd say
I cannot imagine being vegan
Chicken's my wondrous, delicious, lovely
Don't eat chicken and you are a heathen
Devoid of chicken, my stomach's lonely
'Chicken! Chicken!' I cry out in my sleep
Into my dreams now, the chicken does creep.

Jordon Taylor (16)
Hartlepool Sixth Form College, Hartlepool

Her Mother

Her mother is her protection from all,
Her mother looks after her when she's ill,
Her mother gives her courage to stand tall,
Her mother gives her the power and will.

Her mother has raised her from being young,
Her mother helps her if she's in trouble,
Her mothers shows her how to hold her tongue,
Her mother's round when she needs a cuddle.

Her mother supports her when she feels down,
Her mother's courage shows when she's afraid,
Her mother can get rid of any frown,
Her mother helps her, advice ready-made.

Her mother's the one who will always care,
Her mother's the one who is always there.

Christopher Brown (16)
Hartlepool Sixth Form College, Hartlepool

Music

I listen to my iPod
Every single day
Always blaring out
With songs I love to shout!

I listen to my iPod
It helps me to relax.
Tinchy Stryder, he is good
He's a star in the hood.

I listen to my iPod
I feel happy when I do.
Kanye West is the best
He is played over the rest.

Ryan Mangan (12)
Maltings Academy, Witham

Music

M y drum is a lion's roar
U nbelievably loud in the class that is like a jungle
S o I think Alexandra Burke is trying to be like Beyoncé
 I love hearing Paul Potts in the opera
C lassical music is the best because of The Beatles.

Luke Wheeler (13)
Maltings Academy, Witham

Music

M usicians playing music all day
U kuleles strumming away
S ounds going through my ears
 I nstruments made throughout the years
C lassical music is the best, I don't care about the rest.

Ryan Scurr (12)
Maltings Academy, Witham

Music

There's lots of types of music
Like jazz, classical and hip-hop,
And don't forget some others
Like rap and pop.

One of my favourite singers
Is Lady Gaga,
My other favourite singer
Is called Cascada.

We listen to music
When we're in dance,
We also listen to music
On the way back from France.

We have a music lesson
Which is great,
And if you have private lessons
They don't finish late.

I love music
I think it is great,
Now I'd better go
And say goodbye to my mate.

Rhiannon Gladwell (12)
Maltings Academy, Witham

My Music

Music, music, it makes me feel happy,
It makes me feel good,
It makes me smile.

The rhythm of the beat
Makes me stand to my feet,
I want to join in,
I want to dance and sing.

Some music is boring,
Some music is good.
I don't like opera,
I don't think I should.

I like to play the keyboard
And the recorder,
But only when I get
The notes in order.

I love music,
It is so cool,
It makes me relaxed,
Like floating in a pool.

Sophie Hill (12)
Maltings Academy, Witham

Music

Makes me want to sing,
Makes me want to dance,
Music makes me feel sad,
Music makes me feel happy,
Some music repeats in the tune,
That goes over and over.

Music from all different artists,
Beyoncé,
Jay-Z,
And many more.
R 'n' B,
Jazz,
Hip hop,
Rap,
My favourite tunes are remixes.
I'd love to see my favourite artist on tour.

Erin Bristow (12)
Maltings Academy, Witham

Music

Music, music everywhere,
Playing loud for all to hear.

Lots of music can be sung,
Like soul, jazz and pop and rock.

Different music can be played,
The guitar, keyboard, the trumpet, yeah!

Musicians read music all the time,
To see which notes they are on and which words rhyme.

As you see, music is expressed in different ways,
It matters what you like and what you like to play.

Lucy Allen (12)
Maltings Academy, Witham

Music Beats

I can feel the beat,
I can feel the rhythm go through my feet.
I can feel the beat of the drum
Pounding through my ears.
I can see the dancers
Swiftly moving through the air.
I can see happy people smiling.
I can think about famous singers' voices.
I can see and feel the music notes
Jiggle around me.
I love music.
Without it, life would be dead!

Joscelyn Blackmore (12)
Maltings Academy, Witham

Music

M usic is for having fun
U sing your hands to play instruments
S inging to your favourite song
I nside your house listening to the radio
C ome round and dance to the music.

William Harrison (12)
Maltings Academy, Witham

Music, Music

Music, music all around, I love the sound.
I hear it on my way to school,
I hear it with my mates, it's so cool.
As I walk along the corridor,
Oh my God, my mates are dancing like fools.

Music, music all around, I love the sound
On my mp3, iPod or flat-screen TV.
I listen to it all the time
And you don't have to pay a dime.

Music, music all around, I love the sound,
The singers the dancers and the prancers.
R 'n' B, soul, hip hop or rock 'n' roll.
Music, music all around, I love the sound!

Lisa Virgoe (12)
Maltings Academy, Witham

Music

Music makes me want to pop,
I want to dance all around,
Rhythm, blues, soul, hip hop,
I've just got to hear the sound.

Without any background noise,
I kinda feel really sad.
Solo, girl groups and the boys,
Make me go crazy, mad.

Lianne Deal (12)
Maltings Academy, Witham

Music Is Cool

Music is cool,
Pop and jazz,
Make me wanna get up
And dance everywhere.

Music can be calming classics
Or head-banging rock.
Lots of artists
Sing to the melody.

Live concerts cost a lot,
Packed to the rafters,
I hope I can go to one
But not yet, when I'm older.

Adam Abell (13)
Maltings Academy, Witham

Music

Life without music is like
Me without friends.
Life without music is like
Romeo without Juliet.
Life without music is like
Mickey without Minnie.
Life without music is like
A tree with no leaves.
Life without music is like
A sea without fish.
Another way to say that is . . .
Life would be death without music.
Music brings you to life!

Gemma Horseman (12)
Maltings Academy, Witham

Do You Like Music?

As I sit down in music class
I tap to the beat
And bang on the drums,
Then Miss tells me to get to work!

I think of tunes,
I think of a dance,
I think of singing,
Then dance and prance.
Then Miss tells me to get to work!

I picture CDs,
I picture concerts,
My mate playing guitar.
Then Miss tells me to get to work!

Louise Rudd (12)
Maltings Academy, Witham

Music

M aking lovely sounds
U sing different instruments
S he said was worth every pound
 I t seems it's like an ocean sound
C an't tell the difference whether it's quiet or loud.

Kimberley Kisimbo (12)
Maltings Academy, Witham

Music

Music is fast,
Music is slow,
I listen to music
While my car's getting towed.

I sit in jail
Listening to pop,
The jail guard corrects me
And says it's hip hop.

I'm in a concert
Listening to rock,
We shout and scream
To the band, Tick Tock.

Music, I love your songs,
Please,
Please,
Don't get me wrong!

Baileigh Willsher (12)
Maltings Academy, Witham

Music

I love my music
Always as loud as an elephant,
On the stage or in my room,
Sad, happy or full of laughter.

Loads of different instruments
All over the world
Playing loads of different sounds
To make up a beautiful song.

Singing, dancing to the music,
Lots of different notes to play.
Pop, rock, hip hop or what,
I love music!

Ella Martin-Smith (12)
Maltings Academy, Witham

Miley Cyrus

Miley, Miley you always say
Nobody's perfect and that's OK.

Smiley Miley, never change
Because to us you're super strange.

Miley, smiley, always smile
'Cause you know we love your style.

Miley, Miley, I love when you say
Let's go party in the USA!

Weronika Ostrowska (11)
Maltings Academy, Witham

Music Madness

D ancing to the sound of the *beat*
R oaring loud like thunder
U nderstanding how to read music
M usic filling the room with *delight*
S ound beating through the walls.

Kirby Gould (11)
Maltings Academy, Witham

Random Music

The drums go *boom* when you hit the drum.
When I hit the bowl, *ting,* it sounds like a doorbell.
When I hit the keyboard note, the high one,
It sounds like a girl screaming.
When I hear the clock go *tick-tock*
I can make a song out of it.
The violin screeches all day long
And it pierces through my ears.
When I wake up in the morning I hear the birds chirping
And it makes me want to dance all day long.
What can you hear but not touch? Your voice.
Scrunch, I hear people screwing up pieces of paper
And throwing them in the bin.
I hear the bacon sizzling as if it was singing.

Hannah Beilby (11)
Maltings Academy, Witham

Music

I can hear the music
Swishing in the wind.
I can hear the music
Spinning round and round.
I can hear the music
Pushing through the walls.
I can hear the music
Coming out of me!
I can hear the music everywhere,
Even coming out of the birds.
The whole world is full of music,
So you don't have to dream music,
It's already there and ready to play.

Katie Munn (11)
Maltings Academy, Witham

Music

M usic to my ears
U p I jump to the beat of the music
S inging is my lifetime
I always sing and dance
C lapping to the beat.

Tia Coates (11)
Maltings Academy, Witham

The Guess Game

In my home I have an instrument,
Can you guess what I can play?
Makes you happy, makes you relaxed,
When you play, you get attached.
You can blow it, you can push buttons,
You can rock it, you can play it.
When you play it you are calm,
You are happy, you tap your arm.
If you've guessed what I can play,
Well done, you've made my day!

Amy Nevill (11)
Maltings Academy, Witham

Music

Rihanna is OK,
Boyzone rule,
But Britney Spears rocks.
Music makes me feel good,
Makes me tap my feet.
It's got a beat to it,
Makes you feel happy,
All different types,
Music is different.

Nicole Atkinson (11)
Maltings Academy, Witham

Rhythm

The rhythm of the music
Sings to my heart
With its bangs and booms
And other parts.
The songs beat and pump
Like my vein,
Some are soothing,
Others are pains.
When the music stops
I have nowhere to go,
But I always like the sound
Of the beats and flows . . .

Jake McGee (11)
Maltings Academy, Witham

Music

Music, music brightens up my day,
Music makes me dance in lots of different ways.
Music can make me happy or sad,
When I listen to it I feel glad.

When I hear the beat the music makes me move my feet,
Then it makes me want to sing,
I think music is king.
It can make people weep
Or can make them go to sleep!

Lucy Oakman (11)
Maltings Academy, Witham

Death is a sad thing to take,

Always!

Death is a sad thing to take,
But you have to remember the good times always,
For all that is lost is tragic,
But you will always be in our heart.

You were so happy.
When I was feeling blue, you always put a smile on my face.
You tickled me here and there and always made me laugh.
I will always remember you
As a second dad and a great friend.

You always bought me sweets
And always looked after me.
I have poured my heart out in this poem
And I will always remember you.
RIP, Dave Ingelthorpe, you will always be in our hearts,
Always!

Jack Smith (15)
Mecklenburg Pupil Referral Unit, Kingston-upon-Thames

I Don't Like . . .

I don't like cheese or mushy peas
And people who hurt trees.
I don't like spiders and snakes
And other things that make me shake.
I don't like wasps and hornets
Which can be pests
And I don't like it
When I have a poorly chest.
I don't like heights, they give me a fright
And I don't like things that go bump in the night.

This is a poem about things I do not like,
I also don't like pike!

Elizabeth Hunt (11)
Newlands Girls' School, Maidenhead

A Growing Plant

It starts as a tiny seed, small and white in colour,
Put in the ground and watered 'til sound
As it grows taller and taller.
As leaves appear and flowers sprout
And bits of fruit come popping out.
Sunlight and rain make the fruit ripe.
Red, green, yellow and orange types,
Ready to pick, large and juicy,
Soft and shiny, smooth and mushy.
No more fruit as winter arrives,
And the plant goes wrinkly,
Then shrivels and dies.

Danielle Fitt (12)
Newlands Girls' School, Maidenhead

The Secret Life Of A Cat

Have you ever wondered
About the secret life of a cat?
Could she be a ninja
Or a friend of a rat?
A pilot, a police cat
Or even a vet,
Or could she simply be
A family pet?

Iona Collins (12)
Newlands Girls' School, Maidenhead

Full Stop!

At the end of a sentence
There is a full stop. Stop!
When things stop
Things go pop. Stop!
When I'm stuck in a top
People say stop. Stop!
After, I watch my brother
Be in a strop. Stop!
Then, when I see rain
I hear it go *plop.* Stop!
The maid's so embarrassed
She dropped her mop. Stop!

Stop that poem at once.
You really are a dunce.
It's now gonna end
With a full stop. *Stop.*

Yasmin Al-Ghabra (11)
Newlands Girls' School, Maidenhead

Help!

'Help!'
Someone shouts when in trouble,
When someone wants attention,
When it hurts,
Either from the outside
Or from your heart.
'Help!'
Calling when an emergency,
Calling if you want your mum,
Calling when you're stuck.
'Help!'

Madeah Rehman (13)
Newlands Girls' School, Maidenhead

Friends

We're true friends
We're in it till the end
And will never, ever be apart!

We can change the world
With our friendship.
We'll never, ever
Give each other the slip!

Hannah Cheeseman (13)
Newlands Girls' School, Maidenhead

Chicken Rap

I like big wings but I cannot fly,
You other brothers can't deny.
When a girl walks in and I flap my wings
I just can't lift my feet, I've been chopped!
My head has fallen off and I just can't see,
Everybody's laughing at me cos I'm dead.

Lia Cheeseman (12)
Newlands Girls' School, Maidenhead

Autumn

I love autumn because of the leaves
That hang up high in the trees,
Red, orange, brown, yellow and gold,
The brown ones look all crinkly and old, old, old, old.

I love autumn because of the leaves
That hang up high in the trees,
The leaves are crunching
And the rabbits are munching, yum, yum, yum.

I love autumn because of the leaves
That hang up high in the trees,
Soon the leaves will be gone
Before the snow starts to come, come, come.

Hannah-Mae Prodger (11)
St Dominic's School, Brewood

Christmas Eve - Haiku

Stockings being filled
The silent snowflakes falling,
With cookies and milk.

Sydney Larkin (11)
St Dominic's School, Brewood

Sport Is . . .

Sport is fun, sport is cool,
There are loads to pick from, how about you?
Tennis is bouncy,
Swimming is wet,
Cricket is wacky,
Gym is flex.
If you can't pick from them, I'll carry on some more.
Trampolining is jumpy,
Table tennis is ping,
Rounders is batty,
Netball is fling.
You people must be silly if you can't pick a thing.

Emma Hudson (11)
St Dominic's School, Brewood

The Writer Of This Poem

The writer of this poem is as
Slimy as green goo,
Is as small as a thimble
And makes a sound which is *moo*.

The writer of this poem is as
Smelly as some mouldy cheese,
As loud as a lion's roar
And as annoying as a buzzing bee.

Reece Billen (11)
St Dominic's School, Brewood

Bobby, The Rabbit

He's as friendly as a cuddly dog
Who meets you every day at the door.
His ears are like pieces of fluffy fabric,
Waiting to be made into beautiful garments.
He can be as active as a gymnast,
Or as peaceful as a warm fire.
Bobby is as cute as a teddy bear,
And his fur is as soft as a blanket of snow.

Chloe Godfrey (11)
St Dominic's School, Brewood

Pandas

They are as white as snow,
As black as space,
And also very soft.
They're endangered but that doesn't mean
That we should treat them badly.
We shouldn't ruin where they live
Because they aren't human,
But I think they are just like you and me.

Megan Watson (12)
St Dominic's School, Brewood

As Lonely . . .

As lonely as
A picture without any people,
A song without any words,
A television without a screen,
A calculator without any numbers,

A chair without any legs,
A key without a lock,
A door without a handle,
A pen without a lid,

A chat without a mouth,
A dictionary without any words,
An ear without any sound,
An eye without any sight.

Katie Beck (11)
St Dominic's School, Brewood

115

Summer

S apphire sunlight setting at the break of dawn
U sually you will not catch sight of a thorn
M other takes us to the seaside
M y brother and I jump on the water ride
E specially when the sun sets
R equired for the summer's day.

Myrander Coleman (13)
St Dominic's School, Brewood

Ten Little Animals

One outstanding octopus swimming in the sea,
Two talkative tigers terrified they might be seen,
Three threatening tarantulas thinking to trash the treasure,
Four fidgety falcons flying over various fields,
Five flying sparrows fighting for food,
Six silky snakes sliding skilfully past the shrews,
Seven slow snails slime through slippy slides,
Eight eager elephants are eager to elect,
Nine naughty night owls neglecting noise,
Ten teasing turtles terrorising tiny toads.

Kelly Westwood (12)
St Dominic's School, Brewood

All Alone And On My Own

All alone and on my own,
I stare around me.
Books, paper, pens.
I see a light as bright as the sun,
I touch it.
The sensation of happiness and joy overflows,
Then suddenly the room goes black,
I can't wake up!

Katie Randall (12)
St Dominic's School, Brewood

The Rhyme That's Hot!

I never knew about Bust-A-Rhyme
Until my teacher told me that time,
That no matter how bad the rhyme,
I would always win a little prize.

So I decided to give it a shot,
That's how a girl like me
Came up with
A rhyme that's *hot!*

Maneshia Johal (13)
St Dominic's School, Brewood

Friendship

Friendship is a wonderful thing,
Friendship is where people share and care.
When you are down or in trouble, a friend is there.
A good friend should be for life,
To share in good and bad,
In joy and sadness.
When we go our separate ways in life,
We should stay in touch to share our experiences.
When we are apart and feel sad,
We should remember the good times we had.
As we grow older and wiser,
Spare a thought for your special friend,
Up until the very end.

Ellena Thomas (12)
St Dominic's School, Brewood

Love

You are my one and only love
you were sent from Heaven above
I look in your eyes
this is where love lies
as we fly away on the wings of a dove.

Maryan Ahmed (12)
The Crest Girls' Academy, London

The Angry Toad

There was once an angry toad
Who couldn't sing and spent his life on the road
He found a career
But it wasn't that much cheer
He was so miserable he was about to explode.

Sarah Saidova (13)
The Crest Girls' Academy, London

Friends

Friends are those people who touch others' lives
and become part of them.
Friends are those who learn to share in one
another's happiness in their deepest secrets
and their fondest dreams.
A really close friendship doesn't just happen . . .
It takes time to build the kind of trust and
respect that makes a friendship a lasting one.
Friends are those people who touch one
another's hearts and life and make them
brighter and happier as times go by.

Thank you for being you.

Mariam Saklaoui (12)
The Crest Girls' Academy, London

My Limerick!

There once was a student from CGA,
Who got herself in a really big fray,
The police came running,
It was very cunning,
But then got herself in a fray, on May!

Shukri Mohammed (12)
The Crest Girls' Academy, London

Happiness is . . .

Happiness is eating a McDonald's apple pie.
Happiness is drinking a Starbucks latté.

Happiness is melting Galaxy running through your mouth.
Happiness is a marshmallow all nice and fluffy.
Happiness is wishing to fly.
Happiness is laying softly on a beach.

Happiness is going shopping.
Happiness is opening presents.

Happiness is . . . *life!*

Yuser Alsabah (12)
The Crest Girls' Academy, London

Love!

Love is when expressions are revealed
Love is a passion,
Passion that makes you want to sing
Love is dangerous
Love is also very romantic
Love is a dream world
Love is *everything!*

Samra Shaukat (12)
The Crest Girls' Academy, London

Alone

I live in a world where no one cares
I am so alone, sitting on my own
I feel so cold and inside me I know that
there is someone out there for me.

Fathima Hameeya (12)
The Crest Girls' Academy, London

Life ...

All in one land,
living happily ever after,
Then the prince of Maryland comes and destroys our hereafter,
Mummy says, 'No'
Daddy says, 'Run'
People want you to know,
How much life needs in return,
Sisters and brothers, mother and fathers,
Please listen to us and then you'll find out,
this life isn't a joke as it was mentioned by our previous fathers,
And now they just found out,
Now shut your eyes and say goodbye,
as if your life just scrolled by.

Fatima Habib (12)
The Crest Girls' Academy, London

The Girl From CGA

There was a girl from CGA
She was made out of clay
She was always bored
And prayed to the Lord
She wishes she could play.

Osnia Rasooli (12)
The Crest Girls' Academy, London

Match Of The Day

England, Croatia, match of the year,
In my seat, trembling with fear,
The whistle goes, it's all begun,
Off they go, starting to run.

We get the ball,
My heart starts to race,
Theo Walcott,
With his lightning pace.

The ball whips in,
J.T. rises,
Oh my God,
It's full of surprises.

The ball rolls in.

Jack Herrick (12)
Wreake Valley Community College, Leicester

The Comeback

Saturday afternoon Arsenal play,
I sit there anxious hoping it goes their way,
Arsenal one, Tottenham nil,
We're playing football like Brazil,
From left to right we switch the ball,
William Gallas stands strong and tall,
Bacary Sagna number three,
Number 11 RVP,
Abou Diaby is slack in possession,
Tottenham score, that will teach him a lesson,
Francesc Fabregas with his illuminous band,
I stand there tall in the Arsenal stand,
Theo Walcott with his excellent control,
Van Persie turns, shoots *goal!*
The whistle goes, we won't play Tottenham for a while,
I leave the stadium with a giant smile.

Mitchell Gordon (12)
Wreake Valley Community College, Leicester

My House

My house is more like a jungle,
It has monkeys, turtles and pandas
You name it we have it
Monkeys swinging on the chandelier,
Turtles flooding into the house,
Koalas sleeping on the mantlepiece,
There's also a bison in a basin,
Gorillas in the bathtub,
Horses raiding the garden,
Pandas in the pantry.
And there I am crowded around animals,
My house is not a normal house,
It's more like a jungle.

Krishan Rayarel (12)
Wreake Valley Community College, Leicester

Untitled

I have moved house today,
And in this one I want to stay,
I like this one more and more,
There's going to be football galore.
My mum is very tidy,
So it shall stay,
And if anyone goes in there,
They will regret it and pay.
I've got a big new garden,
Filled with colourful flowers.
And big green trees,
They look like towers.
When my goal is set up and ready
I'll be playing every day,
Shooting and scoring,
In this one I want to stay.

Samuel Beaver (13)
Wreake Valley Community College, Leicester

Friends Are Friends!

Friends, friends are so cool,
bullies and badguys are really cruel.
When friends are near me I feel so loved,
when bullies are near me I feel a mug.
Friends stick by me every day,
I just hope they never fade away,
bullies are cruel to me every day,
hopefully one day they might go astray.

Friends are family, I love them so much,
I like to invite them to have a spot of lunch.
They're with me through the good times.
They're with me through the bad.
They're with me through the happy times.
They're with me through the sad.
Friends are family, I love them so much.

Georgia Stuart (12)
Wreake Valley Community College, Leicester

My Family

My family will be the best forever,
they help me through bad and good,
they have helped me and made me happy
for all of my childhood.
But now I'm getting older,
the rest of my family too,
but I know they will love me forever,
they will love the whole family forever,
that includes my sisters and brother too.
Even though we grow up
and go our different ways,
I will have my family with me always.
Through bad and good,
I will remember,
they helped me and made me happy,
for all of my childhood.

Lesley Whitmore (12)
Wreake Valley Community College, Leicester

Making The Right Friends

I am walking along the pavement
Dragging my feet through the leaves,
Then I hear a scream,
A shout,
Voices coming the other way.
A friendly gang of girls,
Eating chips,
Screaming with laughter,
They suddenly stop,
Looking at me from head to toe.
I am thinking whether they will let me join their so cool gang,
I stroll up to them,
The leader stretches out her hand,
I take in a sharp breath,
I know this is the beginning of our friendship.

Isabelle Rose Toon (12)
Wreake Valley Community College, Leicester

League's 11

Peter Crouch does the robot.
David Beckham misses penalties.
Steven Gerrard strikes and hopes, will he score or not?

Up front, strikers score goals.
Midfield players support them.
At the back defenders tackle.
Hard shots are the goalkeeper's problem.

Football is the greatest sport.
It is exhilarating and fast.
It is fun for all the fans.
To see a win at last.

Rowan Kirkland (12)
Wreake Valley Community College, Leicester

Friends

Friends are always there
they love, hug and care.
They were there through the good times
even through the bad.
We have been through a lot
but we got there in the end.
Our relationship will always be there
it will never disappear.

When the skies are grey
you turned them blue
I'm so happy that I have you.

Kirsten Halford (12)
Wreake Valley Community College, Leicester

Downfall Of The Bullies

Those little kids being picked on
by the big boys; they know it's wrong
but no one cares, they pretend not to notice
In fact they are scared, but try not to show this.

Then one day this new girl, she wandered in
and decided to voice what she believed in:
'You boys; you are wrong, you are stupid and mean,
and you teachers; you're the biggest cowards I've seen.
So stop it you boys, and teachers grow up.
Let the children feel happy; instead of choked up.'

'Yes!' cry the students, the big and the small,
'Let's stamp out this bullying once and for all!'
So we're working together to sort them out
to make sure that the children do not want to pout.

Chloe Charlotte Molloson (13)
Wreake Valley Community College, Leicester

My Nanna

My nanna is in her fifties
She's the greatest person I know.
She wears funky Ugg boots
And has been there to watch me grow.

She makes me do my homework
And helps me with what I can't do.
My nanna does most things round the house
But I like to help her too.

I've lived with her since I've been born
In our house at Cambridge Close.
I'd never want to move from here
Cos rain or shine we've been through most.

I love my nanna, she's the best
I hope she's loved like that by the rest.

Shane Roberts (12)
Wreake Valley Community College, Leicester

Names And Fists

Names and fists,
Names and fists,
That's all I ever get,
Cold shoulders and silence,
Cold shoulders and silence,
Is the only thing they do to me,
They ignore me in the corridor,
In the playground and canteen,
In the class they push and shove,
In the line they punch and kick,
When will it end?
I am getting very distressed,
I talked to my mum,
She met with the principal,
It stopped happening all of a sudden,
Now I am happy again.

Alexander Ross (12)
Wreake Valley Community College, Leicester

Girls!

It's not fair being a girl,
The expectations are high,
You cannot lie,
Without being caught.
It's not fair being a girl,
Always having to be clean,
Perfect and pristine,
Like you were bought.
It's not fair being a girl,
You must always look great,
And not ever be late,
Never do anything fraught.
But it's not always so bad,
The attention you get from Dad,
And the shopping makes me glad . . .
That I am a girl!

Sophie Ball (12)
Wreake Valley Community College, Leicester

Friends Forever!

My friends
Are friends forever
They pick me up when I feel down
Cheering me up all through the day
I have trust in you, I hope you do too
They come to my door
Knock, knock, knock
So I come running
I open the door
So we keep on chatting
We can talk for hours and hours
No matter what the weather
Sunny or grey
We're always together
No matter what day
My friends, we'll be friends forever!

Anishaben Patel (12)
Wreake Valley Community College, Leicester

x

Being A Girl

Being a girl
isn't at all fair
there are good times and bad times
when I wish I was there
Playing football, getting muddy
cars, motorbikes and sports
better, higher class jobs
like being head policeman in court
Girls prefer make-up
clothes, perfume and more
Jewellery and dress up
hair products galore
This isn't so fair
can't you see
boys and girls should mix
oh well . . . at least I like being me.

Daniella Agar (12)
Wreake Valley Community College, Leicester

Tonic's Big Day!

There was a loud neigh
and a following bray,
as my legs dug into his side,
we rode in the sand,
and in time I would stand,
as we rode along with the tide,
as he trotted, my heart skipped a beat,
as he tripped on a stone,
and let out a moan,
and I slipped right out of my seat.
I landed on the sand,
and found that Tonic couldn't stand,
I found my phone
and stared at the stones
as I waited for the vet at the end of the line,
I looked at the time
and heard a man's voice.
Had I made the right choice?
He came straight away,
and gave Tonic some hay,
as he healed his leg.
Now he is fine and showing good signs
of recovery.

Mollie Pagett (12)
Wreake Valley Community College, Leicester

Athletics

The gun fires, smoke flies up
My body jumps off the line
I can feel the adrenaline
Pumping through my veins
Straight off the line
I'm in it to win it
I know I am
I'm 4th to 3rd and passing people with flying colours
I am now first, I hope I'll win
I need to keep it up or I will lose
Just before crossing the line
I look at the cheering crowd
I cross the line lunging forward
I took first place, so, so happy
I ran into the 'bag' and bounced off
The crowd loves me!

Adam Hopkins (13)
Wreake Valley Community College, Leicester

I Love My Dog

I try to teach my dog tricks but she's as deaf as a post
As thick as a brick
She owns the house, she's in charge
If you don't do what she says, she'll bite you
You'll go home running
She'll come after you to tell you she's sorry
She'll roll on her back and let you rub
I love my dog.

Brandon Hickling (12)
Wreake Valley Community College, Leicester

The People In My Class

The people in my class!
They mess around so much
Once is a joke
But they go on and on
They never stop
The teachers get so frustrated
So do I
The lessons get so boring
Can't they just stop?
It is so annoying
The people in my class!
When some of them aren't here
The class can be so quiet
I can get on with work
The teachers are calm
The people in my class!

James Hubbard (12)
Wreake Valley Community College, Leicester

Being Me

Being me can be a problem,
I'm different to others you see.
I don't wear what others wear,
I'm happy being me!
I listen to music that isn't popular,
And I don't act like a girl.
I like playing sports,
And I like working at school.
How is that wrong?
I'm from a different background,
My family is different to others.
I don't look like people in magazines,
I don't follow the celebrities.
If I wasn't different, I wouldn't be me,
You see!

Freja Sabine McMurdo (12)
Wreake Valley Community College, Leicester

Me!

As each person went by,
I heard voices in my mind
Telling me that what they said were lies
but as they cornered me again
and beat me up for the 100th time
I could not help thinking that their heart was not kind.

As each day went by
Not a friend had I
Apart from my friend Tom
although he's not real, he makes my wounds heal.

Tom helped me pick up the courage to tell
and now I have a friend called Mel
and everything's how I wanted it to be
Now I feel like me!

Georgia Bargate (12)
Wreake Valley Community College, Leicester

The Ideal Gender

Girls should be beautiful, delicate and sweet,
From the top of their head to the bottom of their feet.
Boys should be sporty, handsome and strong,
Following these rules, is it right, is it wrong?
I believe that you should be free,
No matter what gender you may be.
Girls can be strong and love sports as well,
Whilst boys can be kind and never rebel.
Girls must do washing and stay in all day,
While men can be adventurous and do what they say,
Men must be clever and highly paid,
But women should be loving and are treated like maids.
No,
This is not what I think though.
People should be people no matter who they may be,
Gender means nothing and everyone should agree.

Annie Taylor (12)
Wreake Valley Community College, Leicester

My Best Friend!

My best friend gets bullied by this lad
She comes up to me and claims it's bad.
I tell her to stand up for herself
'Cause I don't understand why he bullies her,
She fits in like a book on a shelf.
Then finally today she stood up for herself and claimed she smacked him
I said, 'Good on yer', he shouldn't have been so full of himself,
He should be learning his lesson by now
But he's not somehow.

Yes it's wrong that she smacked him, and she's still standing up to him.
But I'm proud of her cause she's
My best friend.

Georgia Gatto (12)
Wreake Valley Community College, Leicester

Everyday

I get up in the morning
feeling good,
don't want to go to school,
though I know I should,
walk through the school gates, just standing, waiting,
there I am waiting for the bully to come
and batter my face in,
though they never come,
like they said they would,
I didn't think they would miss,
but I guess they could.
They think I am ugly and quite nerdy,
just cos I am clever, don't make me unsturdy,
don't want to live like this, not anymore!
I guess I do anyway,
this is what life is like for me and others every day.

Lauren Doughty (12)
Wreake Valley Community College, Leicester

The R.A.F

Bang go their guns,
Whoosh go their planes
helping the country
but not in vain.
Saving lives and helping others
trying their best to stop the war,
the wounded and the ill
the rich and the poor
always trying to stop the war.
Boom go the bombs
and *whizz* goes the wind
saving our lives
but not in vain.

Holly Taylor (12)
Wreake Valley Community College, Leicester

Why?

Why does the world have to fight?
Why can't we see that there is just no point?
Why do people murder?
Why do people kill?
Why do people have to die for people we do not know?
Why can't we live forever?

These are all good questions that no one
can answer, but, maybe, maybe one day
somebody will.

Hallie Price (12)
Wreake Valley Community College, Leicester

Birthday Beats

Your birthday is here
The best day of the year
Your presents are in piles
And your cards line up for miles
It's all fun
Until you have to run
All the kids at school will meet
To give you a birthday beat
Your arm will be sore
When they give you more
And when they're done
You'll wish your birthday had never come.

Sam Coupe (13)
Wreake Valley Community College, Leicester

My Friend The Nerd

My friend the nerd,
Is so very, very kind.
But others think she's weird,
'Cause she has a strange mind.
They tell me she's cramping my style,
And I am pretty cool,
But while they're telling me this,
She runs back into school.
I feel really bad,
So I go and look for her,
But I heard a loud scream,
It appeared a fight had occurred.
So I rushed inside,
Looking everywhere,
And there she lay,
Dead without a care.

Victoria Ingram (12)
Wreake Valley Community College, Leicester

Stop!

Stuck in my room for hours on end
all by myself and no one cares
what can I do, they're waiting outside
should I be brave or should I cry?
If I don't stand up to them now it will never end
my heart is racing but no one will listen as
I am now under threat
It's my life -
My dreams, and I don't want anyone to
get in the way of my path to success.
I want to grow up with someone to trust
but nothing helps as everyday they still wait outside my front door,
waiting for me to step outside . . .

Laura Harrison (12)
Wreake Valley Community College, Leicester

Newspaper

Come on newspaper be fair to us too,
List the good things we do.

We aren't all angry and bad,
In my opinion you're terribly sad.

You use the delinquents to say what we are,
To be truthful we don't all steal cars.

Tell the truth and remove our bad name,
If not at least know we're not all the same.

Thomas Brown (12)
Wreake Valley Community College, Leicester

Bullying

Waiting all alone,
With no one there,
Sitting in my room,
With no one that cares,
Wondering if someone will come,
To see how I'm feeling,
What have I done wrong?
The kicking, hitting,
Name calling, shouting,
Is getting into my head,
That I'm not wanted,
No one even cares,
How can it all stop?
I just wish it would,
End!

Lydia Stokes (12)
Wreake Valley Community College, Leicester

Bullies . . .

People that bully
Think they're hard,
But when they're alone they're a piece of lard,
We are feared,
Because bullies are weird,
Bullies should stop,
Because people will call a cop.

Sam Palmer (12)
Wreake Valley Community College, Leicester

My Friend

Even though she's not popular, she has friends
Even though she doesn't wear make-up, she still feels pretty
Even though she's not spoilt, she still has cool stuff
Even though she goes to the library, it doesn't mean she's smart
Even though she doesn't go out much, doesn't mean she doesn't

have a life.

She is who she is!

Abigail Ball (12)
Wreake Valley Community College, Leicester

Bullying

Name calling,
Tripping over,
Taking friends,
The things that upset people,
Looks,
Weight,
Clothes,
Things bullies look for,
Upset,
Sad,
Lonely,
Emotions affect everyone.

Chloe Allen (12)
Wreake Valley Community College, Leicester

Football

You enter the stadium,
What an amazing sight,
You look left and you look right,
You're blinded by the light,
As kick off draws near,
We scream and cheer,
The players come out,
We jump about,
One nil, two nil, three nil, yay,
Will the goals ever stop? Hip hip hooray,
We won the game,
We reached our aim.

Thomas Stanford (12)
Wreake Valley Community College, Leicester

Bullying Is Wrong

They punched her and kicked her
Until she fell to the ground.
She tried to get up
But they pushed her back down.
She went to tell the teachers
But they didn't care.
She went to tell her friends
But none of them were there.
She just wants them to stay away
She's worried what else would happen
If she tried to run away.
She wanted a life with joy and love.
But all she got was beaten up.

Mia Muller (12)
Wreake Valley Community College, Leicester

Detentions

I'm not a fool,
I know why we come to school
but year after year,
I cry a tear,
because of the homework we got,
but I didn't do it because I forgot.
So I got a detention,
and that bought the sad emotion.
I wish detentions were not a real thing,
but that fight I will never win.

Remy Clarke (12)
Wreake Valley Community College, Leicester

The School Bully

He clenched his fist as he closed the door,
He punched me, I hit the floor,
He opened the door and ran away,
I had no doubt he wanted to stay,
I did tell my mum,
She told me to kick him up the bum,
I told my teacher, she told me not to worry,
She said, 'Come on hurry,'
Now I have no problems in the hall,
It turns out he was bullying all the kids at school.

Abbie Doughty (12)
Wreake Valley Community College, Leicester

I May

I may get good grades,
I may look smart,
I may not bully people,
I may not smoke,
I may not do drugs,
But I still think I'm cool.

I may not be good at sport,
I may not have a girlfriend,
I may do all my homework,
I may not have many friends,
But I still think I'm cool.

I may not have had a detention before,
I may have a lot of stars,
I may not be horrible to teachers,
I may have a lot of awards from school,
I may not mix with cool people,
But I still think I'm cool.

You don't have to do things
you don't want to do
to be cool.

David Startin (12)
Wreake Valley Community College, Leicester

Crazy Pets

It was a normal day apart from one thing.

My cat was running round the house,
Meanwhile the budgie ate a mouse.
My dog went bonkers,
While my hog went looking for Willy Wonkers.
The fish jumped out of the bowl,
However my tiger went for a stroll.
The chicken ran up the stairs,
While the rat ate some pears.
My spider ran up the gutter,
But the snake sat in the butter.
My giraffe ate the meat,
But the cow licked my dad's feet.
The cat slept on the bed,
But the lion ate Ned.
So you see pets are very crazy!

Elliott Parker (12)
Wreake Valley Community College, Leicester

My Friend Will

I have a friend called Will,
He's got looks that kill
He's been my friend from primary school,
I think he's really cool.

We used to play for Syston Town,
When we played, everyone used to frown.
Eugene is his nickname,
I think it's really lame.

I hope we're friends for ever,
Never have a fall-out, never, never, never.

Adam Robinson (12)
Wreake Valley Community College, Leicester

Happy Memories

I have a friend called Jess
She lived in the west
America that is
When she flew over
My dad was hung over
And I was looking my best

I fed a kangaroo
In an Australian zoo
It looked at me weird
I thought it had a beard
And it nearly came home with me.

Megan Green (12)
Wreake Valley Community College, Leicester

Want To . . .

She didn't want to know,
She didn't want to hear,
She didn't want her tears,
She didn't want them here,
She wanted to go,
She wanted to shout,
But where nobody could hear,
But where there's nowhere to run,
What's the point 'cus nobody cares.

Jessica Smith (12)
Wreake Valley Community College, Leicester

School Is Bad

School makes me mad because they think I'm stupid.
School makes me angry because none of the teachers trust me.
School makes me laugh when the teacher goes crazy.

Will Pollard (12)
Wreake Valley Community College, Leicester

Football Is The Best Game

Football is the best game,
but other people think it's a shame,
when the crowd screams and shout,
people think, *what's that all about?*
when we score,
the other team thinks, *what a bore,*
but when we win,
everyone will sing,
we will have a laugh,
while the players have a bath,
and we will drink some beer,
and have a massive cheer.

Ben Shaw (12)
Wreake Valley Community College, Leicester

My Missing Crazy Dog

It was a pleasant day,
Suddenly my dog had vanished,
I checked everywhere,
But he was nowhere,
He was a bit bonkers though.

Wait . . . what's that?
It's Jack, my dog!
He is in the back garden,
He was wearing my baseball cap,
He ate some stones,
And found a bone.

I went out to get him,
But he was gone again,
Oh no! He is in the shed,
Now he is in the house,
Looking for a mouse.

Arghh! He let the birds out,
Boom!
Yawn! That was a weird dream!

James Passingham (12)
Wreake Valley Community College, Leicester

Speeding

When cars go speeding by,
It feels like I'm about to die.

60 miles per hour on a 30 miles per hour road,
Why do they do it? There's no reason to squish a toad.

They think they're all cool when then they cause all the damage,
But they're taught a lesson when they have to pay for my wreckage.

The police chase and chase them all day long,
But then they sit there all day, chewing their tongue.

Vishal Mistry (12)
Wreake Valley Community College, Leicester

Football Mania

Football is good, football is bad
if you lose you will be sad.
if the other team boasts you will be mad
but it's only a game, so don't go home and complain
and I know this poem is pretty lame.

Reece Snow (12)
Wreake Valley Community College, Leicester

School

It's boring, it's stupid,
The rules I hate,
The uniform is itchy,
The homework is hard,
I keep telling myself they're going
to pay,
Day after day I keep getting more,
I get detentions, I can't take
it no more.

Davina Patel (12)
Wreake Valley Community College, Leicester

School

School can be good, school can be bad,
But some of the teachers make me so mad.
When you get homework it's best to nip it in the bud,
But if you don't do it, just say it got ruined in the mud.
Maths and English, science and P.E,
Well if anything these are better than R.E.
Humanities is boring but geography can be good,
But if you get stuck with your work ask a teacher, I think you should.
Education helps you achieve your dream,
But when you get that A* you want
I guarantee you'll scream!

Mitchell Paul Beattie (12)
Wreake Valley Community College, Leicester

School

'It's just another detention' I say
But my parents don't see it that way.
Day after day the teachers would shout,
'What are you doing, messing about?'

Days went by, I still brought shame
My parents didn't like it, but it was like a game.
Science, English, maths, they're all really bad,
When I leave school, I'll be so glad.

Too many lessons every day,
Listening to what the teachers say.
After school detention . . . here I come!
Waiting behind me was my angry mum.

Sam Spiers (12)
Wreake Valley Community College, Leicester

Labelling Me!

I like to pose, so I guess I am vain.
I like to wear make-up, so I guess I am fake.
I steal people's boyfriends, so I guess I am mean.
I like to play football, so I guess I am a tomboy.
I like to buy things, so I guess I am rich.
I like chocolate, so I guess I am fat.
I have spots, so I guess I am ugly.
I wear black, so I guess I am a goth.
I wear pink, so I guess I am a Barbie.
I like loud music, so I guess I am a raver.
Why call me names? Because I know what I am like.

Jessica Knighton
Wreake Valley Community College, Leicester

Chocolate

Delicious, delicious, delicious
Chocolate is gorgeous, melt-in-your-mouth tastiness
It is rich, gooey and crunchy
It really is the best thing in the world.

Yummy, yummy, yummy
Chocolate is perfection
It is like magic, truly perfection
It really is the greatest thing.

Addictive, addictive, addictive
Chocolate is different from everything else
It is unique and tasty
It really is the sweetest thing.

Dimple Chauhan (12)
Wreake Valley Community College, Leicester

Chocolate!

I like chocolate
I eat it every day
I eat it for lunch
And I eat it for dinner
Now when I eat it, it makes me a winner
I also thought it made me thinner
Chocolate is good
Chocolate is nice
Heck, I even tried it with rice!

Adam Smith (12)
Wreake Valley Community College, Leicester

Framzi

My friend Framzi will come over by plane,
Although she may have the brain of grain.
And although she may be as sharp as a wooden spoon,
But for me she definitely lights up the room.

Saffia King (12)
Wreake Valley Community College, Leicester

About A Poem

This is a poem,
About a poem,
It is only about a poem,
Because I couldn't think of a poem.

I was going to do it on chocolate,
But nothing rhymed with chocolate,
I was going to do it on my dog,
But I couldn't think of my dog.

This is a poem,
About a poem,
It is only about a poem,
Because I couldn't think of a poem.

Laura Symington (12)
Wreake Valley Community College, Leicester

It's Not Fair

My bike's been locked away
she won't come out to play
my mum fused a chain
put my bike through pain
I want to ride her again.
It's not fair!

Edward Bridge (12)
Wreake Valley Community College, Leicester

The Beautiful Game

They call it the beautiful game,
The ball is round and shines in the sun.
The reason football is the best, is because it is fun.
It's a fun game to play,
It's better than eating hay,
Plus you get some pay.
I love it when we score.
Everyone screams and cheers,
when the lads get beers.
They have lots of fun,
while eating a bun.
They go for an ice bath,
while having a laugh.

Will Kyle (12)
Wreake Valley Community College, Leicester

Football

Football is the beautiful game,
But some people think it's really lame.
Everybody screams and shouts,
But people think, *what's that about?*
When somebody wins the ball,
Everybody suddenly grows tall.
When the final whistle blows,
All the fans rush to go.

Sam Hoey (12)
Wreake Valley Community College, Leicester

Swimming Lesson

Gliding through the water
The coach shouting, 'Go faster!'
You can't go any faster so you take a breath and go again.
You just keep going until you can't feel your legs any more.
You finally get out and feel all relieved
But then you realise that you have to do it all over again.

Michael Hill (12)
Wreake Valley Community College, Leicester

Tears And Fear

C rying
A nger
N ot fair
C areful
E motions
R emedy.

Alexander Trayhurn (12)
Wreake Valley Community College, Leicester

Downhearted!

D epressed
O ppressed
W aiting
N egative
H ateful
E verlasting pain
A rguments
R egretful
T aunted
E verywhere I go I'm scared
D isrespected.

Jade Hewing (12)
Wreake Valley Community College, Leicester

Depression

D ead inside
E verlasting pain
P arents parted
R unning but getting nowhere
E verything reminds me
S uccessfully getting over what happened
S till rattles on in my mind
I need to forgive and forget
O ppressed
N o one understands me.

Philip Bishop (12)
Wreake Valley Community College, Leicester

Cruel Fools!

When I go to school
Students barge past me trying to act cool
But they're just fools
As I walk into the class they start to laugh
Just because I'm new
They make faces behind my back
It makes me sad, but still I leave it,
With fear that they might bully.
Some stand outside as I leave school
They call me names and kick me being cruel.
Even the girls, they pull my hair, chuck my bag on the floor and stamp on it.
I beg, I cry, 'Stop - please - stop, or else I'll die . . .'

Saffiya Kara (12)
Wreake Valley Community College, Leicester

Bullying

Why do I get bullied?
Am I a freak because I don't speak?
Am I ugly because I wear glasses?
Am I stupid because I don't know the answers?
Am I the only one who gets bullied?

Kanela Whitehead (12)
Wreake Valley Community College, Leicester

Head Down – Thumbs Up

Names and words may not hurt,
But try coming into my world, I haven't had my growth spurt.
I get called little midget and mostly little git,
But it doesn't get to me 'cause I miss all the hits.
I dodge all the banging in the mall but mostly in the hall,
They bully me into doing things that I don't want to do,
They make me feel like a big pile of poo!

Jake King
Wreake Valley Community College, Leicester

The Creepy House

I live on the top of a road
In the creepiest house in the world.
It is dark and skeletons are everywhere
and when I stand on the staircase I hear the strangest sound.
I look out of the window and see the most strangest shadow,
it just looks like the vampire in my closet under the stairs.
I tiptoe into where my cat sleeps, on the mat,
I see the cat dead by the vampire under the stairs
I take myself to bed . . .
and never saw life again!

Shanti Leighton (12)
Wreake Valley Community College, Leicester

The Life In School

School is full of different people, look around and
you will see little Year 7s getting lost
but none of them are like me.

The people in school who really annoy me are the
people who just don't care
They pick on people half their size
And that is just not fair

When the bell goes everyone rushes to their lesson
They run and walk
They laugh and scream
but when they all get into class they all turn quiet and
have their hands up in the air, ready to share their answers.

Rebecca Grisenthwaite (12)
Wreake Valley Community College, Leicester

Art Is . . .

Art is an illusion, emotion
this is my way of expression
it's not just an interesting picture
it's a special effect
a way to connect
when drawing a soaring bird
I hope to be heard
it's not just for show
it's my way to glow.
This is my poem . . .

Benjamin James Wilkes (12)
Wreake Valley Community College, Leicester

Just Because

Just because I am bad doesn't mean I can't get a good education.
Just because I can't afford computer games doesn't mean I am poor
Just because I don't do my homework
don't mean I can't spell or read
Just because I don't have any friends
don't mean I am a loner
I am happy
I have friends
I can spell
I like homework
I love books.

Joseph Harper (12)
Wreake Valley Community College, Leicester

Bullying Leaves A Mark

School can be really fun,
But not when the bullies come,
They always steal my lunch money,
They kick my legs, they think it's funny.
They knock my things on the floor,
They hit me, punch me, trap my fingers in the door.
I always dread when lessons end,
They trip me over, it drives me round the bend,
Why do bullies only do it to me?
Will someone eventually make them see
That bullying is a crime?
And this is why I am writing this rhyme.
Bullies really make life sad.
Will they ever see that they are being bad?
Bullying leaves a mark, and I will never forget . . .

Joshua Lester (12)
Wreake Valley Community College, Leicester

Football

Football is my thing
Football is my sport
Football is cheer
Football is fear
Football is goals
Football is rough
Football is tough
But I still like my football
because it's my thing.

Sam Barratt-Lever (12)
Wreake Valley Community College, Leicester

Something Fun

Something fun is . . .
having a laugh,
playing on the park,
not making a mark
Something fun is . . .
making a kite,
having lots to eat,
not sitting on a seat
Something fun is . . .
jumping everywhere,
making lots of sound,
not you never being around
Something fun is . . .
having you near
if you're not, here comes a tear!

Emily Rowlands (12)
Wreake Valley Community College, Leicester

Treats

C hocolate makes my tummy rumble
H oney is made from bees that bumble
O ats are nice and humble
C ustard is nice with crumble
O range sherbet is nice and smooth
L oads of sweets go really far
A ll these sweets in the jar
T offees are nice and they are chewy
E verything here is nice to eat.

Ethan Smith (12)
Wreake Valley Community College, Leicester

Bullies

The bullies always pick on me
Why me?
The bullies always kick me
Why me?

The teacher says, 'Ignore them.'
But it's too hard.
Is it cuz I'm a geek
They call me a freak?

It's not nice, it's not cool
They just make me look like a fool.

Joseph Orme (12)
Wreake Valley Community College, Leicester

My Day

I wake up in the morning
I start yawning
I go downstairs
See what's on the air
I go to school
and act like a fool
I get home
and I start to moan
I have my dinner
So I don't get thinner
then I go to bed
to rest my head.

Liam Asher (12)
Wreake Valley Community College, Leicester

On And On

J ust 'cause I'm tall
O n and on they go
S houting horrible things in my ear
E specially the big boys too
P eople go on and on, making my days miserable
H itting me hurts my heart, not my soul

W orried what they'll do next to me
O n and on they hurt me but
O utstanding, that's what I am
T ough what people think
T ough what people do
O n and on people try and change me but
N othing's gonna change me.

Joseph Wootton (13)
Wreake Valley Community College, Leicester

My Life

My life isn't the life I wanted,
But it's the life I had,
I think my family is mad,
But as I said it's the life I had,
My life feels unwanted,
But I can't change the way I am,
That is my life.

I live with my mum and sister,
I have a dog, a very cute dog,
Not a hog, and I just want to say,
It isn't the life I wanted.

Shaun Steven Brittle (12)
Wreake Valley Community College, Leicester

Crew Begging

They're approaching near, when I'm just standing here.
Her crew make me cry, but shall I run or die?

Everytime I walk by, they come up really sly.
I just wish I wasn't here.

They call me *geek* and *nerd,* but all I hear is the sound *crack.*
The crew aim for my leg.
Then I beg 'Stop', but they just carry on.

They spit on me and kick me.

Another day starts again.

Billy Hall (12)
Wreake Valley Community College, Leicester

208

The Battle Of Confidence!

I've cried so many tears that I just can't cry anymore,
The fear as I walk through the classroom door.
Sitting on my own in the classroom,
Sitting on my own at break times.
I get so angry at people,
I really want to fight back but I haven't got any strength.
I'm too scared, I'm always lonely and always upset.
The bullying, I was sick of it.
I just wanted it to stop.
I stood there shouting, crying.
They listened, they stopped, it all worked.
I spent so much time being sad and all it took was confidence.
I won this battle!

Phoebe Sprigg (12)
Wreake Valley Community College, Leicester

Life Hurts

Life hurts when they start kicking,
and the clock starts ticking.

They steal your school money,
and throw away your honey.

Then my mum had a talk,
and the bullies get on report.

That means you have to be alert,
that's why life hurts.

Alexander James Sharman (12)
Wreake Valley Community College, Leicester

Dust-A-Rhyme - Verses From England

Young Writers Information

We hope you have enjoyed reading this book - and that you will continue to enjoy it in the coming years.

If you like reading and writing poetry drop us a line, or give us a call, and we'll send you a free information pack.

Alternatively if you would like to order further copies of this book or any of our other titles, then please give us a call or log onto our website at www.youngwriters.co.uk

Young Writers Information
Remus House
Coltsfoot Drive
Peterborough
PE2 9JX
(01733) 890066